CONVERSATION STARTERS VOLUME 1

QUESTIONS FOR ROAD TRIPS, DATES, COUPLES, AND ALL OF LIFE'S AWKWARD SILENCES

Conversation Starters Volume 1
*Questions for road trips, dates, couples,
and all of life's awkward silences*

Introduction

First of all, I would like to say thank you for choosing this book. I believe there is a lot of value in having great conversations and I hope you will find this book to be a valuable resource for entertainment and discussion.

There are a lot of different types of questions inside to choose from. Quite a few are small talk questions, many are good for serious discussions, others are thought provoking, and still others are just fun or silly.

I wanted this book to be accessible for as many people and for as many situations as possible. So just skim through the book. I'm sure you'll find questions that will allow you to start a great conversation with almost anyone.

What's the difference between Vol. 1 and Vol. 2?

The only difference between volume one and volume two is that the questions are different. The format is the same for both books and even the introduction is the same in both books. I wanted people to be able to pick up volume one or volume two and have the same great experience. So if you enjoyed one volume you will definitely enjoy the other.

How are the questions organized?

They aren't. I could have classified them by topic or by the seriousness of the question, but I decided to put them in random order. I did this for two reasons.

First of all, I didn't want to classify them by topic because I want people to discover interesting questions about topics they might not normally choose to talk about.

Secondly, classifying questions by the seriousness of the question is too subjective. Even questions designed for small talk can lead to a serious discussion.

Plus I think you'll find the randomness of the questions more entertaining. If you don't like a question or topic, just go to the next question. It will be totally different.

How many questions are there?

If you look at the headings, there would appear to be 230, but in fact there are quite a few more. Many of the questions are actually a set of questions around a general topic.

So without any further delay, let's get started with the questions.

Conversation Starter Questions

QUESTION 1

Does motivation come from inside a person or from their environment? What motivates you? Why?

QUESTION 2

What do you think about most when you are lying in bed before you go to sleep?

QUESTION 3

Would you like to open your own business? If so, what type of business would you like to open? If no, why not?

QUESTION 4

Dueling was common in the past. If dueling was made legal, would it solve any problems? What problems would it create?

QUESTION 5

What is a fashion trend now that in 10 years people will look back on and laugh about? Do you know anyone who follows that fashion trend?

QUESTION 6

Describe your best friend. How long have you been friends? Why are they your best friend?

QUESTION 7

The only people who need privacy are people doing something illegal. Do you agree or disagree? Why? Do you think people have the right to privacy? How about convicted criminals?

QUESTION 8

Very intelligent people are often not very good at fitting in, why do you think this is? Give some examples of very intelligent people who break this stereotype.

QUESTION 9

Do you think that digital cameras will totally kill film cameras? Why or why not?

QUESTION 10

What is the funniest show on television?
What makes it so funny?

QUESTION 11

Who deserves to be tipped but isn't? Why do
they deserve to be tipped? Is there a job
where it is customary to tip but shouldn't be?

QUESTION 12

More and more education is being done
online. How will this change education?
Should a university education be free? Why or
why not?

QUESTION 13

Do you think smart phones increase or decrease productivity? Why or why not? What might smart phones do in the future that will dramatically increase productivity?

QUESTION 14

Are cities good or bad for the environment as a whole? Why?

QUESTION 15

Have you ever had a flying dream? If not, would you like to? Have you ever been dreaming and woken up and couldn't move?

QUESTION 16

If you see a homeless person on the street asking for money, what is the first thing that goes through your mind?

QUESTION 17

What in your life wastes the most amount of your time?

QUESTION 18

What are some ethical dilemmas you have faced?

QUESTION 19

Do you know anyone who talks in their sleep? What do they say? Does anyone in your family sleep walk?

QUESTION 20

Why do some people try illegal drugs and others don't?

QUESTION 21

Where did you spend your last vacation? What did you do?

QUESTION 22

Do you think that some people are more productive because of genetics or how they were raised? What can people do to become more productive?

QUESTION 23

What is the first thing you notice about a person? Why do you think you notice that first? What does it tell you about the person?

QUESTION 24

When did you get your first email address? Do you still have or remember the address?

QUESTION 25

How do different cultures think about beauty differently?

QUESTION 26

What are some things that are new now but might be valuable antiques in the future?

QUESTION 27

Have you ever tried drawing, painting, sculpting, or something else artistic? Were you/are you good at it?

QUESTION 28

What music do you listen to when you are sad? What do you listen to when you want to relax?

QUESTION 29

How do you define the word "home"? Is it where you live, where your family lives, or where you grew up? Why?

QUESTION 30

What kind of new hobby would you like to try? Why?

QUESTION 31

If aliens came and met with your country's government, what do you think would happen? How would the government respond?

QUESTION 32

Most electronics are black, silver, or white. Why do you think this is? How do you customize how your gadgets look?

QUESTION 33

In public, how much affection is too much?

QUESTION 34

Do you think a person's job determines who they are? Why or why not? Can a person's job change their personality?

QUESTION 35

What is the purpose of news companies in society? Do you think they accomplish this purpose?

QUESTION 36

What are some of the advantages and disadvantages of books vs. movies?

QUESTION 37

Do you think computers will ever be able to think for themselves or have "real" intelligence? What do you think will happen if computers become self-aware?

QUESTION 38

What would your ideal house look like on the inside and outside?

QUESTION 39

How stressed are you? What causes the most amount of stress in your life?

QUESTION 40

What age, in your opinion, is too young to get married? Why is that age the cutoff?

QUESTION 41

What is the best snack to eat during a movie? Why is it so good? Do you only eat that snack when you watch movies?

QUESTION 42

Why do you think humans are the only creatures on the planet that have pets? Or do you think some animals might have pets too?

QUESTION 43

What is the most romantic, exciting, or boring movie you have ever seen?

QUESTION 44

What country do you think as a whole is the most creative? Why is that country so creative?

QUESTION 45

How are celebrities today different than celebrities 50 years ago?

QUESTION 46

What are some different types of crazy diets you have heard of? Have you tried any of them?

QUESTION 47

What do you think of modern art? Which do you prefer classical art or modern art?

QUESTION 48

How can countries help foster more inventors? Can a government increase creativity in its population?

QUESTION 49

Talking to strangers used to be common. How often do you start a conversation with people you don't know? Do you think we should talk to people we don't know more often?

QUESTION 50

Do you believe in luck or do you think it's all just chance? Why?

QUESTION 51

What will influence the future of medicine the most? Genetics? Cybernetics? Chemistry? Some other field of study?

QUESTION 52

How can science help society? Does it hurt society in any way?

QUESTION 53

Should news be more entertaining or more informative? Why?

QUESTION 54

About how many hours of TV do you watch every day? Do you think you watch too much TV?

Question 55

Do you think animals can feel empathy? If so, which animals? If not, why are humans the only ones?

Question 56

What is the most worthwhile thing a person can do with their free time?

Question 57

What website do you spend the most time on? Is it time well spent or a waste of time?

QUESTION 58

Do you think the invention and rise of computers has been a good thing or a bad thing? Why?

QUESTION 59

What kind of humor do you find the most funny? Can you give an example of it?

QUESTION 60

Is it more important to teach students world history or their country's history? Why?

QUESTION 61

Do you think aliens have ever visited earth? Why do you think so? If aliens did come to earth, would they have a reason to stay or avoid earth?

QUESTION 62

How will technology change glasses? What might be some benefits or drawbacks of that change?

QUESTION 63

What were some of the books you had to read for school? Did you enjoy any of them? Why or why not?

QUESTION 64

Are games good for you or bad for you? Are there some that are better for you than others? Give some examples.

QUESTION 65

What piece of tech do you really want that doesn't exist yet? (Flying cars, teleportation, etc.) What would you do if you had it?

QUESTION 66

Are there any diseases that you think humans could eliminate if we tried?

QUESTION 67

What makes a good interior for a restaurant? Office? Home? Classroom?

QUESTION 68

If we could clone dinosaurs and bring them back to life, would you want to? How about cloning ancient humans, Neanderthals, or other early hominids?

QUESTION 69

What is the scariest movie you have ever seen? Why was it so scary?

QUESTION 70

What are some hobbies that improve a person's life? Do all hobbies improve people's lives? Why or why not?

QUESTION 71

What do you think of people who refuse to take modern medicine and will only use natural remedies? How about parents who will only allow their children to use natural medicines?

QUESTION 72

Has medicine ever saved your life?

QUESTION 73

What kind of news stories interest you the most? What was one recent news story you were very interested in?

QUESTION 74

Would you want to have a clone of yourself? Why or why not? Keep in mind your clone would start as a baby.

QUESTION 75

What are the three most important pieces of advice a parent can give their child?

QUESTION 76

Are there any drugs which are legal but should be illegal? Why? Are there any illegal drugs that should be made legal?

QUESTION 77

Do you enjoy having responsibilities? Why or why not?

QUESTION 78

What is the craziest example of a luxury item you have heard of?

QUESTION 79

Are good family members or good friends more important? Why?

QUESTION 80

Which character from a book or movie are you most like?

QUESTION 81

Are you good at saving money? If so, when did you learn how to save money? If not, why not?

QUESTION 82

Have you ever pressed "send" then immediately wished you hadn't?

QUESTION 83

Do you agree or disagree with the proverb, "Money is the root of all evil"? Why?

QUESTION 84

Do you feel sorry for famous people being bothered by paparazzi or do you think that's part of their job?

QUESTION 85

Can intelligence be measured? If so, what is the best way to measure it? Are there any problems with the current way intelligence is measured?

QUESTION 86

What advice would you give to someone who wants to make the world a better place?

QUESTION 87

Do you prefer cities or the countryside? Why?

QUESTION 88

If you could go back in time and give yourself some advice, what would you tell your younger self?

QUESTION 89

Have you met someone you hated right away, even though you didn't know them? Why?

QUESTION 90

What is the first thing you think of when you think of three?

QUESTION 91

How important is creativity for success in business? Do you think businesses value or foster creativity as much as they should?

QUESTION 92

What would be the most amazing keychain ever?

QUESTION 93

What do you think the future of cars will be?

QUESTION 94

What are some of the possibilities of technology in clothing?

QUESTION 95

What makes you unique?

QUESTION 96

Is it better to build concrete block buildings that are cheap, easy to build, easy to repair, and all look the same or more expensive unique buildings that might be less functional? Why?

QUESTION 97

Do you have any bad habits? What are they?
How bad are they?

QUESTION 98

Do you think a four day work week would be
a good idea? What would be some of the
ramifications of a four day work week?

QUESTION 99

What kinds of personality traits do you hate?

QUESTION 100

What is the greatest threat to your safety? Is your answer based on statistics or what you feel?

QUESTION 101

What is the most interesting thing you have ever found?

QUESTION 102

Should humans try to protect natural wonders? If humans protect natural wonders, are the wonders still natural?

QUESTION 103

What is the rudest thing someone can do during a movie? What other annoying things do some people do during movies?

QUESTION 104

Is fashion important or not important? Why or why not?

QUESTION 105

Where is the best place to eat near where you live? Why is it so good?

QUESTION 106

What is the most intelligent animal? Why do you think it's the most intelligent?

QUESTION 107

What do you think has been the most important new invention in the last 50 years?

QUESTION 108

At what age do you think someone becomes responsible for his or her actions? Why?

QUESTION 109

What traditional values are not important or not necessary now?

QUESTION 110

What is your favorite appliance, electronic device, or piece of furniture in your home?

QUESTION 111

What are some ways people can invest their money? What is the worst investment someone can make?

QUESTION 112

Do you collect anything now? How about when you were a child? Did your parents collect anything as you were growing up?

QUESTION 113

How many hours of sleep should people get every night? How many hours of sleep do you get every night? What is the longest you have ever slept?

QUESTION 114

If you could only read one book for the rest of your life, what would it be? Why would you choose that book?

QUESTION 115

If you could make a movie, what would it be about?

QUESTION 116

How much empathy do you feel towards other people? Do you think it's possible to be too empathetic?

QUESTION 117

Is it more important for mothers to stay at home with the kids or go to work to earn more money for the family? Why?

QUESTION 118

How has technology changed the way we consume news? How has it changed how the news is reported?

QUESTION 119

Do you think that some people are destined to meet or is it all random chance? Why?

QUESTION 120

Have you ever met someone from a mafia group? What mafia groups have you heard of? Where are they located?

QUESTION 121

How does technology help creativity? Can technology hurt creativity?

QUESTION 122

Are you a cat person, dog person, or do you like both, or neither of them? Do you think whether a person likes cats or dogs says a lot about their personality?

QUESTION 123

Why are some dangerous drugs legal, like alcohol and cigarettes, while other drugs are illegal? What legal drugs do you use?

QUESTION 124

Are pets good to have around children? What is the best pet for a child to have? Why?

QUESTION 125

What man-made wonders would you like to visit? Why?

QUESTION 126

Do you eat different foods or drink different beverages depending on the season or weather? Give some examples. What is your favorite seasonal food or drink?

QUESTION 127

How long do you want to work before you retire? Do you think you will still want to work even after retiring?

QUESTION 128

What is the best email you have ever received? Do you remember how you reacted when you received it?

QUESTION 129

What two sports would you like to combine into a new sport?

Question 130

What is something that other people value highly that you don't value at all?

Question 131

In the future, will we be able to add machines to a large percentage of our body to improve it? Would you replace parts of your body with machines? Why or why not?

Question 132

What are some examples of good and bad manners in other countries?

QUESTION 133

Who should pay for a person's health care, the government, the sick person, or their workplace?

QUESTION 134

Who is an author that you like? Why do you like their books?

QUESTION 135

How is communication changing between people? How will people communicate in the future?

QUESTION 136

What do you think of arranged marriages?

QUESTION 137

What is the fastest you have gone in a car?
How did it make you feel?

QUESTION 138

What kinds of things do parents have to give
up when they have children? What are some
of the benefits of having children?

QUESTION 139

Do you prefer to have many friends or just a few that are close? What are the benefits of having just a few close friends? How about the benefits of having many friends?

QUESTION 140

Would you jump into a deep river to save a drowning animal? Why or why not?

QUESTION 141

Do police make you nervous or do they make you feel safe?

QUESTION 142

Look up the new 7 wonders of the world. Have you been to any of them or do you know someone who has been to any of them? What do you know about each one?

QUESTION 143

Where is the best place to be in summer? How about winter?

QUESTION 144

How is showing love different now from in the past? Do you think people in the past were more or less romantic?

QUESTION 145

Should people try to make sure their children have easy lives with few difficulties or make sure their children face challenges? Why?

QUESTION 146

How much aid should governments give to other countries? When is it appropriate to send aid to another country?

QUESTION 147

Can you predict whether a kid will grow up to be a criminal or not? If so, how? If not, what are the biggest causes of criminal behavior?

QUESTION 148

How many of the seven ancient wonders besides the pyramids can you name without looking them up? If it was possible to travel back in time, which one would you most like to visit?

QUESTION 149

What is your earliest memory?

QUESTION 150

What are some hobbies that are typically thought of as just for boys? How about just for girls? Do you think that boys and girls are naturally better at certain hobbies?

QUESTION 151

How clean is your house? Are you a very organized person? Do you have a lot of decorations in your home or is it bare?

QUESTION 152

Which was better for you: elementary school, junior high school, or high school? Why?

QUESTION 153

How will medicine and health care change in the future?

QUESTION 154

If you could have three wishes that would come true after you died, what would they be?

QUESTION 155

If you could recommend just one website, what would it be?

QUESTION 156

What is the longest amount of time you have gone without sleep? How did you feel? Why couldn't you sleep?

QUESTION 157

Which would you prefer to visit, a human built wonder or a natural wonder? Why?

QUESTION 158

If we could clone famous people like Albert Einstein or Leonardo Da Vinci, should we? Do you think they would be as successful if they were brought back as clones?

QUESTION 159

What are the three best movies you have ever seen?

QUESTION 160

Compare games your parents played with games you like to play. Are games in the present better or worse than games in the past?

QUESTION 161

Do you think people today work harder than their parents? Why or why not?

QUESTION 162

Talk about the differences between how you and your parents use a computer. Do children use computers in a different way than you or your parents?

QUESTION 163

What was something that you were really good at when you were a kid but aren't good at now?

QUESTION 164

What are some strange hobbies you have heard of?

QUESTION 165

What is the biggest thing you have done to help a friend?

QUESTION 166

What kind of qualities do you look for in a friend? What is the best way to make new friends?

QUESTION 167

If you could save ten people you don't know by killing one person with your bare hands who you don't know, would you? How about if you knew the ten people or the one person?

QUESTION 168

What is the biggest change most people experience in their lives? How does that change usually affect a person?

QUESTION 169

Do you think your parents ate healthier food at your age than you do? How about your grandparents?

QUESTION 170

Do you think that organic food is much better than non-organic food or are they about the same?

QUESTION 171

Do you think it is a good idea for governments to fund man-made wonders for their countries? Why or why not?

QUESTION 172

What do you hope will happen today?

QUESTION 173

What is the best way to prevent crime?

QUESTION 174

Do you have any good luck charms or rituals? If so, when do you use them? If not, why not?

QUESTION 175

What cars do you think look the best? What cars look ridiculous?

QUESTION 176

Why do you think that humans started living in cities rather than just small communities? Was it a good decision for humans to start living in cities?

QUESTION 177

Do you think people can communicate with ghosts and spirits? What do you think of mediums who claim to be able to communicate with spirits?

QUESTION 178

Tell your best or worst travel story.

QUESTION 179

What do you think about the fashion industry? What would you change about it?

QUESTION 180

What is the unhealthiest meal you can think of? Would you eat t?

QUESTION 181

What is the grossest thing you have seen someone do?

QUESTION 182

Do you think society is losing its values? How have values changed in society?

QUESTION 183

Do you think people should give money to homeless people? Why or why not? Do you give money to the homeless?

QUESTION 184

Which sense would you like to improve if possible?

QUESTION 185

Are there any fashion trends in the past you followed but are embarrassed about now?

QUESTION 186

Some people say that poorer societies have stronger values than richer countries. Do you agree? Why or why not?

QUESTION 187

Can a book change the world? How? Can you think of any examples of this happening? Could you write a book that would change the world?

QUESTION 188

Do you think we have or can have any other senses? Would it be possible to develop other senses with technology? If so, what kinds? If not, why not?

QUESTION 189

Talk about how technology has changed in your lifetime.

QUESTION 190

Where do you go or what do you do when you want to be alone?

QUESTION 191

Have you ever hand-written a letter and sent it to someone? If no, why not? If yes, when was the last time you sent a hand-written letter?

QUESTION 192

What is the most interesting holiday or festival you have heard of?

QUESTION 193

What is the strangest thing you have heard of people collecting? Why do they collect them?

QUESTION 194

What movie had the biggest impact on your childhood? Do you think it helped shape who you are today?

QUESTION 195

Would you risk your life to save a friend? How about a stranger?

QUESTION 196

Is addiction to illegal drugs a disease or a crime?

QUESTION 197

How should members of a family support each other as they get older?

QUESTION 198

How many people should a person date before getting married? Why?

QUESTION 199

How often do you lie? When is it okay to lie?

QUESTION 200

What is the next challenge you want to overcome in your life?

QUESTION 201

Why do you think some people fall out of love while others stay in love?

QUESTION 202

What sci-fi movie will the future be like? Why do you think so?

QUESTION 203

Do you believe there is any other intelligent life in the universe? If so, what do you think aliens might look like? If not, why not?

QUESTION 204

What is the most interesting period in history? Why?

QUESTION 205

Do you think it's better to have children when you are older or younger?

QUESTION 206

What were some of the bands you really loved when you were younger but are embarrassed by now?

QUESTION 207

Have you ever been to a really disgusting hotel? Did you stay or leave? What is the worst hotel or hostel you have stayed at?

QUESTION 208

Some people say that marriage is an outdated custom. Do you agree or disagree? Why?

QUESTION 209

Is there a part of your appearance that you are very proud of? (Eyes, fashion sense, hair, etc.)

QUESTION 210

Do you think it is better to save money or invest money? Why?

QUESTION 211

What do you think about the health care
system? How could it be improved?

QUESTION 212

Are you good at keeping secrets? Why or why
not? Do you like knowing and finding out
secrets? Why?

QUESTION 213

What super power would you like to have?
Why? If you had a super power, would you be
a super hero or a super villain? What would
your name be?

QUESTION 214

What is the angriest sounding language? What is the most romantic sounding language? How many languages can you say "hello" in?

QUESTION 215

What do you think about couples that adopt children from different countries? What qualities make a couple or a person qualified to adopt a child?

QUESTION 216

Do you think immigrants to a country work harder than people born in that country? Why or why not?

QUESTION 217

What is your go to song to get pumped up to do something?

QUESTION 218

What makes a leader great?

QUESTION 219

What animal best represents you? Why?

QUESTION 220

What are the three best restaurants you have ever eaten at?

QUESTION 221

Give an example of a technology that has made the world worse. How has it made the world worse? Have there been any benefits from it?

QUESTION 222

Have there been any failures that made your life better?

QUESTION 223

What values did your parents stress as you were growing up? Are there any values your parents tried to make you follow but you weren't good at following?

QUESTION 224

What do the clothes someone wears say about that person? What do your clothes say about you?

QUESTION 225

Is technology making our ability to remember better or worse? Give some examples.

QUESTION 226

Some people believe that the harder you work, the luckier you are. Do you agree or disagree? Why?

QUESTION 227

If you had $10,000 to improve your home, what would you spend it on?

QUESTION 228

What are some things your family did in spring when you were a child? Talk about a particularly pleasant memory.

QUESTION 229

What are some strange pets you have heard of people owning? What exotic animal would you like to have as a pet?

QUESTION 230

What is something you wish you had learned when you were younger?

The End

I want to extend my sincerest thanks for buying this book. I truly hope you found the questions useful and enjoyable.

If you did enjoy the book and want to spread the word, I would very much appreciate it if you took the time to leave a review on Amazon.

Leaving a review on Amazon helps people find the book and helps me write more books. Think of it as spreading the gift of great conversation to a stranger. Hopefully they will pick up a copy of this book and start some of their own thought provoking conversations.

23893083R00048

Printed in Great Britain
by Amazon